About Mastering Basic Skills—Grammar:

D1551051

Welcome to Rainbow Bridge Publishing's Mastering Basic Skills—Grammar series, grade two. Mastering grammar skills builds confidence and enhances a student's entire educational experience. This workbook is designed to help students understand and master sentence construction and fundamental grammatical principles. It both reinforces classroom skills and gets students well on their way to reading and writing independently and competently, and it is ideal for use during or after school.

By making a connection between their previous language experience and the ideas in the text, students realize they have already learned a number of key grammar concepts. Based on NCTE (National Council of Teachers of English) standards and core curriculum, this workbook helps students understand basic sentence patterns, beginning with subject and predicate. They build on this foundation by completing exercises and games that teach parts of speech, proper nouns, plurals, pronouns, verb tense and number, agreement, sentence types and basic punctuation. By continually relating workbook concepts to their existing knowledge, students learn to recognize correct grammar and construct their own sentences.

This workbook holds the students' interest with a mix of humor, imagination and instruction. The diverse assignments teach proper use of adjectives and adverbs while also giving students something fun to think about—from the Parthenon to the platypus. As students complete the workbook, they will be well prepared to master additional language skills related to word choice, meaning, intent and audience.

Nothing is more basic to a solid education than reading and writing. This workbook helps students enhance both skills, strengthening students' confidence, helping them enjoy language and ultimately encouraging them to read and write on their own.

Rainbow Bridge Publishing
www.summerbridgeactivities.com
www.rbpbooks.com

Table of Contents

Name _____   Date _____

◇ **Start Here!**

Put these sentences in order. Look for clues to help you.

Example: fun to fly. would be It = It would be fun to fly.

1. to fly with wings. tried Man

_____

_ _

_____

2. a air hot balloon. first flew in Man

_____

_ _

_____

3. North Carolina. The first flown airplane was in

_____

_ _

_____

4. sent The Soviets into space. the first man

_____

_ _

_____

5. the moon. was Neil Armstrong the first man on

_____

_ _

_____

Name _____ Date _____

◇ Start Here!

Write a subject for each sentence.

The <u>subject</u> tells what a sentence is about.

Example: The class went on a picnic. (<u>Class</u> is the subject.)

---

1 _____

    _____ had a picnic in the park.

2 _____

    _____ is the best food in the basket.

3 _____

    _____ eat at a table in the lunchroom.

4 _____

    _____ sit together with their class.

5 _____

    _____ is on the menu at the restaurant.

6 _____

    _____ works at the restaurant.

7 _____

    _____ is my favorite treat.

8 _____

    _____ bakes them fresh every morning.

Name _____   Date _____

◇ **Start Here!**

Write a predicate to complete each sentence.

The <u>predicate</u> tells what the subject is or does.

Example: The grandfather clock fell over. (<u>Fell</u> <u>over</u> is the predicate.)

---

1. Haley's wristwatch _____.

2. The alarm clock _____.

3. My mom's kitchen timer _____.

4. The grandfather clock in the living room _____.

5. Dad's pocket watch _____.

6. The flower in the garden _____.

Name _____ Date _____

◇Start Here!

Fill in a subject or predicate for each sentence.

1 At school today we ___had art class___ .

_____

2 _____ gave us three pieces of clay.

_____

3 My friend Garth _____ .

_____

4 _____ threw away his statue.

_____

5 The teacher _____ .

_____

6 _____ came in and showed us how to smooth the edges with a little water.

_____

7 She _____ .

_____

8 _____ set them on the counter to dry.

Name _____   Date _____

◇ Start Here!

Answer each question with a telling sentence. Make sure it begins with a capital letter and ends with a period (.).

A <u>telling</u> <u>sentence</u> tells about someone, someplace, or something.

Example: My name is Matt.

---

1 What is your last name? _____

2 How many children are in your family? _____

3 Do you have any pets? _____

4 What do you like to eat? _____

5 Where do you live? _____

6 What do you like to do after school? _____

Name _____ Date _____

> ◇ **Start Here!**
>
> Pretend I have taken a trip to the moon. Write five questions you would like to ask me about my trip. Remember to begin with a capital letter and end with a question mark (?).

Asking sentences are questions.

Example: Is the moon really made of green cheese?

1 _____

_____

2 _____

_____

3 _____

_____

4 _____

_____

5 _____

_____

Name _____   Date _____

◇ Start Here!

Fill in a period (.) if the sentence is a telling sentence. Color it yellow. Fill in a question mark (?) if it is an asking sentence. Color it pink.

1 A hedgehog is one of my favorite animals ___.   Do you know why _____

When a hedgehog is afraid it rolls itself into a ball _____   You can't even see

its legs or its face _____

2 Have you ever seen a hedgehog _____   You probably won't see one in the

winter _____ They hibernate in the winter _____   Do you know what

hibernate means _____   It means to sleep all winter long _____

3 Can you believe a hedgehog has 5,000 spines like a porcupine _____

> Hedgehogs are cute, but I don't think I would want to pet one!

Name _____   Date _____

◇ **Start Here!**

Write an exclamation you might say when you read each sentence.
Remember to end with an exclamation point (!).

A sentence that shows you are feeling happy, mad, excited, or afraid is called an
<u>exclamation</u>.

Example: There's a giant spider on my desk!

---

1 The goliath bird-eating spider is as big as a dinner plate.

_____

- -

_____

2 A group of orb weaver spiders can make a web as large as a bedsheet.

_____

- -

_____

3 An ordinary house spider can run across the floor at one mile per hour.

_____

- -

_____

4 The female black widow kills her mate.

_____

- -

_____

Name _____   Date _____

◇ Start Here!

Fill in a period (.) if the sentence is a telling sentence. Fill in a question mark (?) if it is an asking sentence. Fill in an exclamation point (!) if it is an exclamatory sentence.

1. The Egyptians wrote on a plant named papyrus more than 5,000 years ago

   _____ (.) (?)   The paper we use was invented by the Chinese 2,000 years

   ago _____ (.) (?)

   There sure is a lot to know about paper!

2. Did you know wasps make paper _____ (!) (?)

   They make it from chewed up wood and plants _____ (.) (?)

3. Millions of trees are cut down every year to be made into paper _____ (?) (!)

   Now many people use recycled paper _____ (?) (.) Using recycled paper

   helps save forests _____ (.) (?)

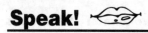
Name _____ Date _____

◇ Start Here!
Draw a line from the word on the left to the best ending on the right.

A <u>command</u> <u>sentence</u> tells someone to do something.
Example: Go brush your teeth.

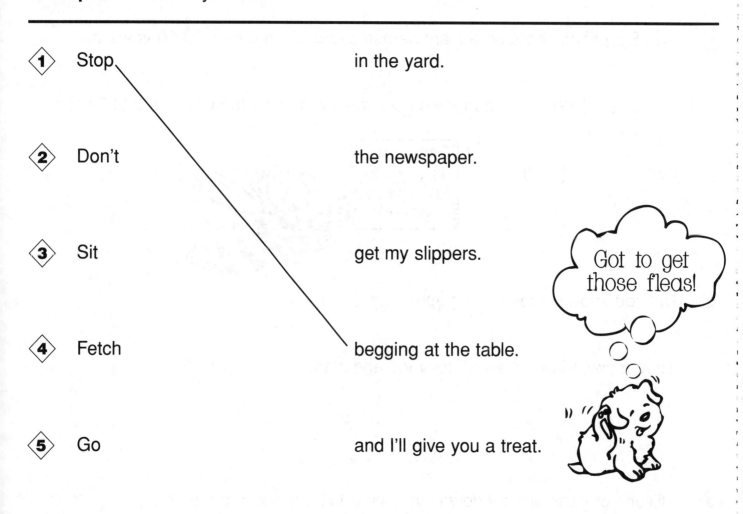

① Stop   in the yard.

② Don't   the newspaper.

③ Sit   get my slippers.

④ Fetch   begging at the table.

⑤ Go   and I'll give you a treat.

⑥ Stay   sit on the couch.

⑦ Roll   over and play dead.

 Matt's Marvelous Idea: Can you guess what this page is about?

© **Rainbow Bridge Publishing**   www.rbpbooks.com   reproducible   **MBS—Grammar Grade 2**

Name _____ Date _____

◇ Start Here!

Write a command sentence for each event.

1 Megan's ball rolls into a busy street. What do you tell her?

Don't run in the street.

2 Your brother spills his lemonade. What do you tell him?

_____

_____

3 It's late, but your cat wants to play. What do you tell it?

_____

_____

4 Rob has your mitt. What can you tell him nicely?

_____

_____

5 Your friends run off to play ball. What can you tell them?

_____

_____

6 Jason knocks on your bedroom door. What can you say?

_____

_____

Name _____   Date _____

◇**Start Here!**

List all the nouns you find in this picture.

A <u>noun</u> names a person, place, animal, or thing.

Examples: teacher   park   horse   book

slide

The Doughnuts Were Delicious

Name _____ Date _____

◇ Start Here!

It begins with a capital letter. Circle the proper nouns in the sentences below.

A <u>proper</u> <u>noun</u> is the name of a person, place, or thing.

Examples: Amanda　　　Wyoming　　　Bible

1 Miss Jones took us to the bakery.

2 On the way we passed North High School.

3 We walked along Maple Street.

4 Tyler Anderson sang a song.

5 The name of the bakery is Perfect Pastries.

6 We told them we were from Jackson Elementary.

7 The owner, Larry, gave us all free doughnuts.

8 He also gave us each a carton of Meadow Gold milk.

Name _____   Date _____

◇Start Here!

Add <u>s</u> to make the nouns below plural. Write the new word.

<u>Plural</u> <u>nouns</u> name more than one person, place, or thing. To make some nouns plural, add <u>s</u>.

Examples:

day	coin	student	teacher
days	coins	students	teachers

1   dog   _dogs_

2   cat

3   book

4   desk

5   microscope

6   sailboat

7   crocodile

8   glider

9   circuit

Name _____   Date _____

◇**Start Here!**
Draw a line to match the singulars and plurals.

If a noun ends in <u>s</u>, <u>sh</u>, <u>ch</u> or <u>x</u>, make it plural by adding <u>es</u>.

Examples: bus   peach
                 buses   peaches

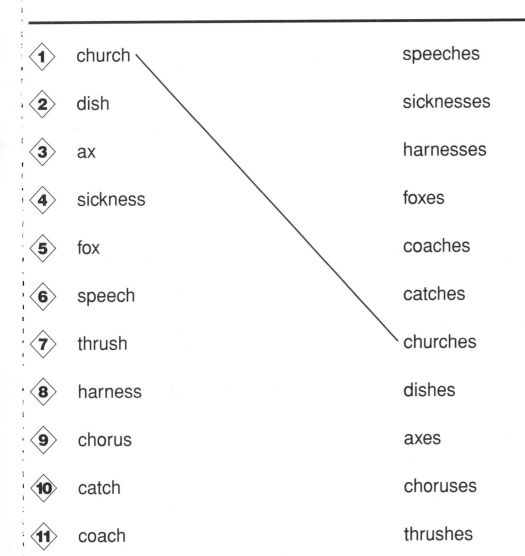

① church   speeches

② dish   sicknesses

③ ax   harnesses

④ sickness   foxes

⑤ fox   coaches

⑥ speech   catches

⑦ thrush   churches

⑧ harness   dishes

⑨ chorus   axes

⑩ catch   choruses

⑪ coach   thrushes

© Rainbow Bridge Publishing   www.rbpbooks.com   reproducible   **MBS—Grammar Grade 2**

Name _____   Date _____

◇Start Here!

Fill in the correct plural noun.

1   There are many different kinds of (map) __maps__.

2   Some show (hill) _____ and (lake) _____.

3   Some show (street) _____ and (building) _____.

4   (Cross) _____ might mean (church) _____.

5   Mapmakers are called (cartographer) _____.

6   Maps for sailors show water (depth) _____.

7   (Atlas) _____ are entire books of maps.

8   A map of the school might show where different (class) _____ are held.

 Matt's Marvelous Idea: Draw a map showing how to get from your house to your school.

Name _____   Date _____

◇**Start Here!**
List all the verbs you can find in this picture.

Most <u>verbs</u> show action.

Examples: walk   study   yell

ride
_____
- -
_____
- -
_____

Name _____   Date _____

◇**Start Here!**

Write in the correct verb for the sentences below.

Some <u>verbs</u> do not show action. Instead, they tell about a person, place, animal, or thing.

Examples: am   is   are

The book <u>is</u> here. I <u>am</u> a student.

---

1. The Statue of Liberty _____is_____ in New York.

2. The Great Wall of China _____ 2,514 miles long.

3. When I stood on the Great Wall, I yelled, "I _____ king of the world!"

4. Many famous structures _____ in Paris.

5. Two of them _____ the Notre Dame Cathedral and the Eiffel Tower.

6. Stonehenge _____ in England.

7. The Pyramids _____ tombs made of stone.

Name _____   Date _____

◇Start Here!

Circle the correct verb in the sentences below.

Use <u>was</u> for singular subjects and <u>were</u> for plural subjects.

Examples: Miss Jones <u>was</u> not here yesterday.

The other teachers <u>were</u> here.

1. Thomas Jefferson (was) were) the author of the Declaration of Independence.

2. Andrew Jackson and Dwight Eisenhower (was, were) famous soldiers.

3. Two recent presidents (was, were) Ronald Reagan and Bill Clinton.

4. Abraham Lincoln (was, were) president during the Civil War.

5. George Washington (was, were) our first president.

6. Calvin Coolidge (was, were) the thirteenth president.

7. Five presidents (was, were) from Ohio.

Name _____   Date _____

◇ Start Here!

Circle the correct verb.

Present-tense action verbs that tell about one person, place, animal, or thing have <u>s</u> or <u>es</u> added to the end. Present-tense action verbs that tell about more than one thing stay the same.

Examples: The teacher <u>reads</u> her book.

The students <u>read</u> their books.

---

1. Tornadoes (form), forms) funnels of wind.

2. Rain (fall, falls) every day in some places.

3. A weather vane (point, points) into the wind.

Singing in
the rain...

4. Some people (believe, believes) dancing brings rain.

5. Miss Jones (teach, teaches) us about the weather.

6. We (know, knows) the South Pole is very cold.

7. Each day, someone (give, gives) a weather report.

8. We all (make, makes) weather predictions.

Name _____   Date _____

◇ Start Here!

Add ing to each base word. Write the new word.

Many verbs have an ing form.

Examples: pick   picking

_____

wait   _waiting_   walk   _____

read   _____   drink   _____

sleep   _____   jump   _____

Write the correct ing verbs for these sentences.

1. I am (learn) _____ about raccoons.

2. The raccoons were (sleep) _____ in the winter.

3. Now they are (eat) _____ almost everything in our yard.

4. Raccoons are always (search) _____ for food.

5. They have been (hunt) _____ outside at night.

6. The raccoon babies were (follow) _____ their mother.

7. We won't be (keep) _____ the raccoons as pets.

Name _____   Date _____

◇ **Start Here!**

Make up your own story by choosing past-tense verbs from the box.

To make regular action verbs past tense, add <u>ed</u>.

Examples: work   play

            worked   played

---

walked	landed	wished	leaped
jumped	marched	painted	dreamed
floated	fished		

Yesterday I ‾leaped‾ into my secret garden. I sat down on my

_____ favorite huge leaf. A giant butterfly flew by. I _____ that I could fly

_____ too. Suddenly I could. I _____ through the air. Then I

_____   _____

_____ in a pool of water. I was so happy, I _____ all

day long.

Name _____ Date _____

◇ Start Here!

Circle the correct verb.

1. Miss Jones (teach, **teaches**) us about Australia.

2. There (is, are) many interesting animals there.

3. Last week, we (enjoy, enjoyed) reading about koala bears. They (eat, eats) leaves.

4. Wombats go out (look, looking) for food at night.

5. We saw kangaroos that (jumped, jumps) high.

6. A dingo is a wild dog. It (hunt, hunts) rabbits.

7. Emus are tall birds. They cannot (fly, flies).

8. The platypus (lay, lays) eggs.

Kangaroos are some of my favorite animals!

Name _____ Date _____

◇**Start Here!**

Circle the correct noun or verb.

1 Miss Jones (call, (calls)) the solar system Earth's backyard.

2 The (student, students) like to read about the different planets.

3 The solar system (was, were) formed billions of years ago.

4 I (am, is) most interested in Mercury.

5 The (objects, object) between Mars and Jupiter (is, are) called asteroids.

6 We (was, are) learning about four giant planets.

7 (It, They) (am, are) Jupiter, Saturn, Uranus and Neptune.

Name _____ Date _____

◇**Start Here!**

Choose the correct noun or verb from the box and write it below.

formed	Sunspots	reaches	A flare
is	look	gasses	change

1. The sun ____is____ really a star.

2. Burning _____ make up most of the sun.

3. The sun _____ five billion years ago.

4. Light from the sun _____ Earth in eight minutes.

5. You should never _____ directly at the sun.

6. _____ are cooler areas on the sun.

7. Solar cells _____ sunlight into electricity.

8. _____ is a huge explosion.

Name _____   Date _____

◇ Start Here!
Draw a line between the present and past tense of each verb. Use a different color crayon each time.

Some past tense verbs do not end with <u>ed</u>. These are called <u>irregular</u> <u>verbs</u>.

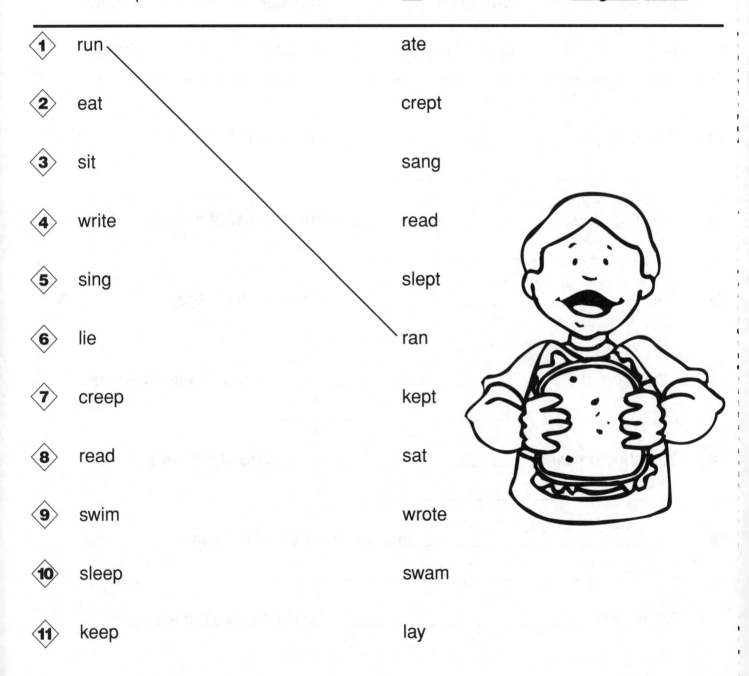

①	run	ate
②	eat	crept
③	sit	sang
④	write	read
⑤	sing	slept
⑥	lie	ran
⑦	creep	kept
⑧	read	sat
⑨	swim	wrote
⑩	sleep	swam
⑪	keep	lay

Name _____ Date _____

◇ Start Here!

Use the irregular verbs and other words to make your own story.

read	took	got	fast swimmer	said
won	wrote	brought	beautiful singer	
He	She	sang	swam	ran

Yesterday, I ___read___ a story. Once upon a time, there was a

_____ _____

_____ _____. At the age of five, this person

_____ _____

_____ lessons. _____ loved to practice every day. This

_____ _____

person _____ very well and _____ a contest. This per-

_____ _____

son _____ a trophy and _____ it to school. The stu-

_____

dents _____ to the auditorium. "Hurray for the winner," they

_____

_____,

Name _____   Date _____

◇ Start Here!

Write two adjectives for every toy that needs to be put in the toy chest.

<u>Adjectives</u> are words that describe a person, animal, place, or thing.

Example: small blue ball   (<u>small</u> and <u>blue</u> would be adjectives.)

black _____

_____

_____

_____

_____

_____

_____

_____

_____

_____

_____

_____

_____

_____

Amazing Amazon

Name _____ Date _____

◇ Start Here!

Draw a leaf around the adjectives in each sentence.

Example: My ⟨favorite⟩ jungle is the Amazon.

---

① The mysterious Amazon Jungle is in Brazil.

② It is the biggest jungle in the world.

③ This massive jungle is called a rain forest.

④ All year long it is hot and wet.

⑤ The Amazon River is the longest river in South America.

⑥ Many monkeys live there.

⑦ A rain forest has tall trees and thick creeping vines.

⑧ There are thousands of unusual plants and animals in the Amazon.

⑨ The Amazon's anaconda snake is longer than 25 feet and weighs 500 pounds.

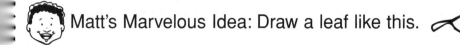 

Matt's Marvelous Idea: Draw a leaf like this.

Name _____ Date _____

◇ Start Here!

Write the <u>er</u> and <u>est</u> words for each word.

Adjectives that compare two things often end in <u>er</u>. Adjectives that compare three or more things often end in <u>est</u>.

Examples: My house is <u>big</u>. His house is <u>bigger</u>. Your house is the <u>biggest</u>.

cold   colder   coldest

tall

big

late

smart

low

fat

slow

cute

I am the mightiest grammar student in the land!

 Matt's Marvelous Idea: Find out who or what is the world's tallest building, tree, or person.

Name _____   Date _____

◇ **Start Here!**
Write the correct article next to each food.

A and an are adjectives we call articles. Use an when the next word starts with a vowel sound. Use a when the next word starts with a consonant sound.

Examples: an orange   a doughnut

1 _____ an _____ apple   _____ pickle

2 _____ olive   _____ muffin

3 _____ tomato   _____ salad

4 _____ milk shake   _____ hamburger

5 _____ egg   _____ drumstick

6 _____ tangerine   _____ ice cream cone

7 _____ slice of pie   _____ soda

8 _____ sandwich   _____ banana

9 _____ mango   _____ omelet

We Are a Club

Name _____   Date _____

◇ **Start Here!**

Circle the pronouns.

Nouns name a person, place, animal, or thing. A <u>pronoun</u> is a word that takes the place of a noun. Some pronouns are <u>I</u>, <u>you</u>, <u>she</u>, <u>he</u>, <u>it</u>, <u>they</u> and <u>we</u>.

1   (I) have a clubhouse in the backyard.

2   It is up in that huge oak tree.

3   You can climb up there on a rope ladder.

4   I am the president, and Caron is secretary.

5   We are best friends.

6   She has a brother named Aaron.

7   He and Kevin are in the club.

8   I wanted to name the club Sherry's.

9   They didn't like that name.

10 Can you think of a name for the club?

 Matt's Marvelous Idea: Can you name the subject of each sentence?

©Rainbow Bridge Publishing   www.rbpbooks.com   reproducible   **MBS—Grammar Grade 2**

Name _____ Date _____

◇ **Start Here!**

Replace each crossed out subject with a <u>subject</u> <u>pronoun</u> from the pronouns box.

| I | he | she | it | they | we |

1. ~~Our class~~ _____ went to the recycling plant.

2. ~~Mrs. Marcus~~ _____ told us about pollution.

3. ~~Pollution~~ _____ can be garbage, chemicals, or smog.

4. ~~These~~ _____ can spread over land, air, and water.

5. ~~Pollution~~ _____ kills some fish and birds.

6. ~~Recycling~~ _____ makes new things from garbage.

7. ~~Rob and I~~ _____ will help stop pollution.

8. ~~The man who runs the plant~~ _____ said it's our earth!

Name _____   Date _____

◇ Start Here!

Choose a pronoun from the pile of wood to fill in each blank.

Pronouns like <u>me</u>, <u>us</u>, <u>them</u>, <u>him</u>, <u>her,</u> and <u>it</u> take the place of a person, place, animal, or thing. These pronouns follow action words or words like <u>to</u>, <u>of</u>, or <u>for</u>.

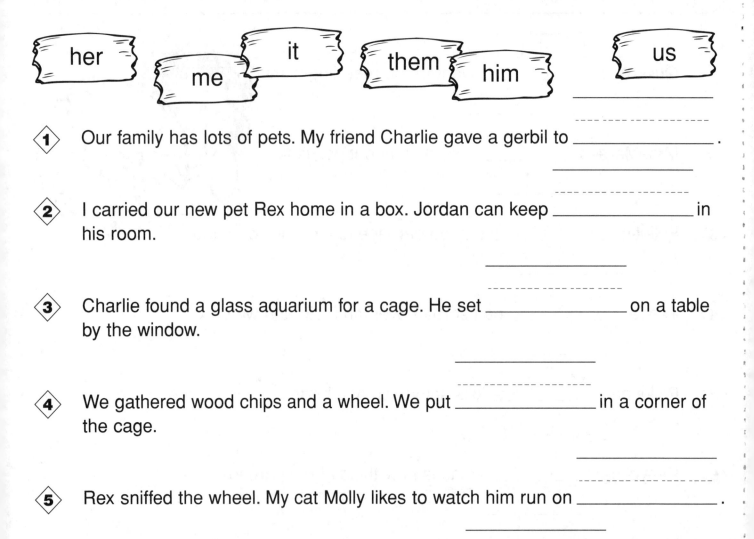

her   me   it   them   him   us

1. Our family has lots of pets. My friend Charlie gave a gerbil to _____ .

2. I carried our new pet Rex home in a box. Jordan can keep _____ in his room.

3. Charlie found a glass aquarium for a cage. He set _____ on a table by the window.

4. We gathered wood chips and a wheel. We put _____ in a corner of the cage.

5. Rex sniffed the wheel. My cat Molly likes to watch him run on _____ .

6. "Don't touch Rex, Molly!" we yelled. We chased _____ from the room.

7. "I really think Rex is cute. Look, he's smiling at _____ ."

Name _____ Date _____

◇ Start Here!
Read "Matt's Marvelous Idea" at the bottom of the page. Then highlight each sentence that has a pronoun and underline the pronoun.

Example: Old buildings are interesting to <u>me</u>.

---

① Since long ago people have built wonderful things like palaces, bridges, and towers.

② Romans built the aqueducts that carried water to them.

③ A pharaoh built the Great Pyramid of Cheops.

④ The people buried him deep down inside.

⑤ The Parthenon was built for a goddess.

⑥ This temple was constructed for her 2,300 years ago.

⑦ The Statue of Liberty sits in New York Harbor.

⑧ The country of France gave it to us.

⑨ Sarah is going to show me all these wonders in her <u>Book</u> of <u>Knowledge</u>.

Matt's Marvelous Idea: <u>Highlight</u> means to color over very lightly.

Let the Games Quickly Begin

Name _____   Date _____

◇ **Start Here!**

Fill in the puzzle with the adverb for the underlined word.

Adverbs describe verbs. Many adverbs end in ly and tell how something is done.

Examples: softly   proudly

Across

⟨1⟩ Cross country skiers are swift. They glide _____.

⟨2⟩ The ice skater is slow to get off the rink. She gets off _____.

⟨4⟩ It is sad when the games are over. We watch _____.

⟨6⟩ Runners who carry the torch are proud. They run _____.

⟨7⟩ The ski runs are groomed and neat. Those runs are _____ groomed.

⟨8⟩ A ski jumper made a bad turn. She was _____ hurt.

⟨9⟩ The bobsledders practice so they will be quick. They race _____.

Down

⟨1⟩ The soft breeze blows the winner's flag. It waves _____.

⟨3⟩ The crowd shouts a loud hurrah. They shout _____.

⟨5⟩ The crowd is quiet when the torch is lit. The crowd sits _____.

⟨8⟩ Most Olympians are brave. They compete _____.

Name _____   Date _____

Wow! This looks like quite a puzzle!

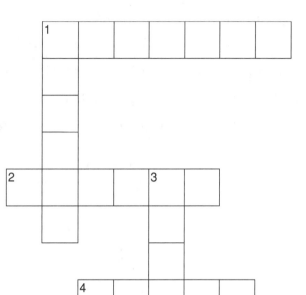

Yeah, but we can solve it!

Name _____   Date _____

◇ **Start Here!**

Add 's to make the nouns possessive. Complete a phrase by choosing words from the box. Make funny phrases. **Example:** Jack = Jack's long nose

A <u>possessive</u> <u>noun</u> shows that someone or something owns or has something. You make a noun possessive by adding 's.

Example: The student's coat was orange.

---

huge claws	sore toe	old skin	huge trunk
nice haircut	wad of gum	long tail	scary face
painted fingernails	pretty dress	pair of glasses	sharp teeth

1   the teacher   teacher's _____

2   the cat

3   Bob

4   Tracy

5   my mom

6   my pet snake

7   the elephant

8   the monster

Name _____ Date _____

◇Start Here!
Write the correct pronoun in the sentences. Add a capital letter if needed.

A <u>possessive</u> <u>pronoun</u> takes the place of a possessive noun.

Examples: The <u>teacher's</u> desk is neat.

<u>Her</u> desk is neat.

---

his   her   our   their   its   your   my

1   My friends and I have a club. We like _____ our _____ club.

2   Miss Jones has a brown purse. She lost _____ purse.

3   Jared has a dog. _____ dog is named Spot.

4   I went to visit relatives. _____ grandpa was there.

5   I like playing at your house. _____ mom always makes cookies.

6   My parents like movies. <u>Star</u> <u>Wars</u> is _____ favorite.

7   My brother has a big truck. _____ tires are also big.

©Rainbow Bridge Publishing   www.rbpbooks.com   reproducible   **MBS—Grammar Grade 2**

Name _____   Date _____

◇ **Start Here!**

Make your own list to complete each phrase. Each list should include at least three items. Remember to add commas.

Use a <u>comma</u> to separate items in a list.

Example: We ate grapes, apples, oranges, and lemons.

---

① At the zoo we saw lions, emus, and _____ .

② In class we studied _____ and _____ .

③ My friends are _____ and _____ .

④ My favorite foods are _____ and _____ .

⑤ Some planets are _____ and _____ .

⑥ Lying in my bed, I can see _____ and _____ .

Name _____   Date _____

◇ Start Here!

When you write a date, put a comma between the day and year. Insert commas in these sentences.

Example: She was born on March 12, 1993.

---

1   Abraham Lincoln was born in Kentucky on February 12 1809.

2   The Declaration of Independence was signed on July 4 1776.

3   Martin Luther nailed his famous list on a church door on October 31 1517.

4   Joan of Arc was killed on May 30 1431.

Write dates correctly as you answer these questions.

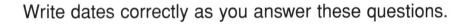

1   When were you born? _____

2   What is today's date? _____

© Rainbow Bridge Publishing   www.rbpbooks.com   reproducible   **MBS—Grammar Grade 2**

Name _____ Date _____

◇**Start Here!**

Insert a comma at the right place in these sentences.

When you combine two sentences to form a <u>compound</u> <u>sentence</u>, put a <u>comma</u> before the connecting word.

Examples: Connecting words: and   but   or   yet   so

         I went to the store. I bought some candy.

         I went to the store, and I bought some candy.

1. Our teacher brought a treat and we ate it all.

2. I searched my pack but I couldn't find my pencil.

3. I got sick so I went home.

4. I sang and I danced.

I bet you can do these problems in a snap!

5. He is going to the movie or he is going to the park.

6. She is only fifteen yet she is going to college.

7. My class is fun and I like it.

8. My teeth hurt so I went to the dentist.

9. I can't play the piano but I can play the violin.

Name _____   Date _____

◇ Start Here!

Make compound sentences by using a comma and a connecting word.

Connecting words: and   but   or   yet   so

Example: The ocean is big. It is full of animals.

The ocean is big, and it is full of animals.

---

1 The swordfish is fast. It can swim 60 miles per hour.

_____

_____

2 A finback whale is big. It is not as big as a blue whale.

_____

_____

3 A jellyfish is interesting. It can sting you.

_____

_____

4 Moray eels hide in cracks. They hide in caves.

_____

_____

5 Many birds like the shore. It's a good place to see them.

_____

_____

Answer Pages

Page 3
1. Man tried to fly with wings.
2. Man first flew in a hot air balloon.
3. The first airplane was flown in North Carolina.
4. The Soviets sent the first man into space.
5. Neil Armstrong was the first man on the moon.

Page 4
Answers will vary. Each sentence should start with a subject and a capital letter.

Page 5
Answers will vary. Each sentence should end with a complete predicate.

Page 6
Answers will vary.

Page 7
Answers will vary but should be complete sentences.

Page 8
Answers will vary. Each should be a complete question.

Page 9
Yellow:
1. A hedgehog is one of my favorite animals.
   When a hedgehog is afraid it rolls itself into a ball.
   You can't even see its legs or its face.
2. You probably won't see one in the winter.
   They hibernate in the winter.
   It means to sleep all winter long.
Pink:
1. Do you know why?
2. Have you ever seen a hedgehog?
   Do you know what hibernate means?
3. Can you believe a hedgehog has 5,000 spines like a porcupine?

Page 10
Answers will vary.

Page 11
1. The Egyptians wrote on a plant named papyrus more than 5,000 years ago. The paper we use was inventedby the Chinese 2,000 years ago.
2. Did you know wasps make paper? They make it from chewed up wood and plants.
3. Millions of trees are cut down every year to be made into paper! Now many people use recycled paper. Using recycled paper helps save forests.

Page 12
1. Stop begging at the table.
2. Don't sit on the couch.
3. Sit and I'll give you a treat.
4. Fetch the newspaper./ Go get the newspaper.
5. Go get my slippers./ Fetch my slippers.
6. Stay in the yard.
7. Roll over and play dead.

Page 13
Answers will vary, but they should be complete commands.

Page 14
shovel, dog, helmet, girl, shoe, shirt, slide, boy, bike, sand, shorts, ball, basket, wheel, cloud, sidewalk, glasses, hair, etc.

Page 15
1. Miss Jones
2. North High School
3. Maple Street
4. Tyler Anderson
5. Perfect Pastries
6. Jackson Elementary
7. Larry
8. Meadow Gold

Page 16
1. dogs
2. cats
3. books
4. desks
5. microscopes
6. sailboats
7. crocodiles
8. gliders
9. circuits

Page 17
1. church, churches
2. dish, dishes
3. ax, axes
4. sickness, sicknesses
5. fox, foxes
6. speech, speeches
7. thrush, thrushes
8. harness, harnesses
9. chorus, choruses
10. catch, catches
11. coach, coaches

Page 18
1. maps
2. hills, lakes
3. streets, buildings
4. Crosses, churches
5. cartographers
6. depths
7. Atlases
8. classes

Page 19
ride, run, dig, play, bounce, scratch, spin, etc.

© Rainbow Bridge Publishing   www.rbpbooks.com   reproducible   MBS—Grammar Grade 2

Answer Pages

Page 20
1. is
2. is
3. am
4. are
5. are
6. is
7. are

Page 21
1. was
2. were
3. were
4. was
5. was
6. was
7. were

Page 22
1. form
2. falls
3. points
4. believe
5. teaches
6. know
7. gives
8. make

Page 23
waiting, walking
reading, drinking
sleeping, jumping
1. learning
2. sleeping
3. eating
4. searching
5. hunting
6. following
7. keeping

Page 24
Answers will vary.

Page 25
1. teaches
2. are
3. enjoyed, eat
4. looking
5. jumped
6. hunts
7. fly
8. lays

Page 26
1. calls
2. students
3. was
4. am
5. objects, are
6. are
7. They, are

Page 27
1. is
2. gasses
3. formed
4. reaches
5. look
6. Sunspots
7. change
8. A flare

Page 28
1. run, ran
2. eat, ate
3. sit, sat
4. write, wrote
5. sing, sang
6. lie, lay
7. creep, crept
8. read, read
9. swim, swam
10. sleep, slept
11. keep, kept

Page 29
Answers will vary.

Page 30
Answers will vary.

Page 31
1. mysterious
2. biggest
3. massive
4. hot, wet
5. longest
6. Many
7. tall, thick
8. unusual
9. longer

Page 32
colder, coldest
taller, tallest
bigger, biggest
later, latest
smarter, smartest
lower, lowest
fatter, fattest
slower, slowest
cuter, cutest

Page 33
1. an apple, a pickle
2. an olive, a muffin
3. a tomato, a salad
4. a milk shake, a hamburger
5. an egg, a drumstick
6. a tangerine, an ice cream cone
7. a slice of pie, a soda
8. a sandwich, a banana
9. a mango, an omelet

www.rbpbooks.com   reproducible   MBS—Grammar Grade 2

Answer Pages

Page 34
1. I
2. It
3. You
4. I
5. We
6. She
7. He
8. I
9. They
10. you

Page 35
1. Our class—We
2. Mrs. Marcus—She
3. Pollution—It
4. These—They
5. Pollution—It
6. Recycling—It
7. Rob and I—We
8. The man—He

Page 36
1. us
2. him/it
3. it
4. them
5. it
6. her/it
7. me

Page 37
(Give students credit for recognizing the possessive pronouns <u>his</u> and <u>her</u>.) Highlighted sentences and pronouns:
2. them
4. him
6. her
8. it
9. me

Pages 38–39
Across
1. swiftly
2. slowly
4. sadly
6. proudly
7. neatly
8. badly
9. quickly

Down
1. softly
3. loudly
5. quietly
8. bravely

Page 40
the teacher's
the cat's
Bob's
Tracy's
my mom's
my pet snake's
the elephant's
the monster's
Other answers will vary.

Page 41
1. our
2. her
3. his
4. my (or our)
5. Your
6. their
7. Its

Page 42
Answers will vary.

Page 43
1. February 12, 1809
2. July 4, 1776
3. October 31, 1517
4. May 30, 1431
1–2. Answers will vary.

Page 44
1. Our teacher brought a treat, and we ate it all.
2. I searched my pack, but I couldn't find my pencil.
3. I got sick, so I went home.
4. I sang, and I danced.
5. He is going to the movie, or he is going to the park.
6. She is only fifteen, yet she is going to college.
7. My class is fun, and I like it.
8. My teeth hurt, so I went to the dentist.
9. I can't play the piano, but I can play the violin.

Page 45
Various answers are possible, but the following answers allow use of all five connecting words.

1. The swordfish is fast, and it can swim 60 miles per hour.
2. A finback whale is big, but it is not as big as a blue whale.
3. A jellyfish is interesting, yet it can sting you.
4. Moray eels hide in cracks, or they hide in caves.
5. Many birds go to the shore, so it is a good place to see them.

© Rainbow Bridge Publishing   www.rbpbooks.com   reproducible   MBS—Grammar Grade 2

Rainbow Bridge Publishing
Certificate
of Completion

Awarded to

_____

for the completion of

Mastering Basic Skills

_____   _____
Publisher's Signature   Parent's Signature

Summer Bridge Activities™

Title	Price
Grade P-K	$12.95
Grade K-1	$12.95
Grade 1-2	$12.95
Grade 2-3	$12.95
Grade 3-4	$12.95
Grade 4-5	$12.95
Grade 5-6	$12.95

Summer Bridge Middle School™

Title	Price
Grade 6-7	$12.95
Grade 7-8	$12.95

Summer Bridge Reading Activities™

Title	Price
Grade 1-2	$6.95
Grade 2-3	$6.95
Grade 3-4	$6.95

Summer Journal™

Title	Price
Summer Journal™	$4.95

Summer Dailies™

Title	Price
Summer Dailies™	$4.95

Summer Traveler™

Title	Price
Summer Traveler™	$4.95

Math Bridge™

Title	Price
Grade 1	$9.95
Grade 2	$9.95
Grade 3	$9.95
Grade 4	$9.95
Grade 5	$9.95
Grade 6	$9.95
Grade 7	$9.95
Grade 8	$9.95

Reading Bridge™

Title	Price
Grade 1	$9.95
Grade 2	$9.95
Grade 3	$9.95
Grade 4	$9.95
Grade 5	$9.95
Grade 6	$9.95
Grade 7	$9.95
Grade 8	$9.95

Skill Builders™

Title	Price
Phonics Grade 1	$2.50
Spelling Grade 2	$2.50
Vocabulary Grade 3	$2.50
Reading Grade 1	$2.50
Reading Grade 2	$2.50
Reading Grade 3	$2.50
Math Grade 1	$2.50
Math Grade 2	$2.50
Math Grade 3	$2.50
Subtraction Grade 1	$2.50
Subtraction Grade 2	$2.50
Multiplication Grade 3	$2.50

Connection Series™

Title	Price
Reading Grade 1	$10.95
Reading Grade 2	$10.95
Reading Grade 3	$10.95
Math Grade 1	$10.95
Math Grade 2	$10.95
Math Grade 3	$10.95

Mastering Basic Skills™

Title	Price
Grammar Grade 1	$5.95
Grammar Grade 2	$5.95
Grammar Grade 3	$5.95
Word Problems Grade 1	$4.95
Word Problems Grade 2	$4.95
Word Problems Grade 3	$4.95
Word Problems Grade 4	$4.95
Listening Skills Grade 1	$4.95
Listening Skills Grade 2	$4.95
Listening Skills Grade 3	$4.95

Math Test Preparation™

Title	Price
Math Test Prep Grade 1	$10.95
Math Test Prep Grade 2	$10.95
Math Test Prep Grade 3	$10.95

First Step Spanish™

Title	Price
Colors/Shapes	$5.95
Alphabet/Numbers	$5.95

Place
Proper
Postage
Here

**Rainbow Bridge Publishing
PO Box 571470
Salt Lake City, Utah 84157**

Keeping Children Busy, Happy, and Learning During the Summer and Beyond!